Here Come the

a FableNotes©

written and created
by Marin Marka

Illustrations
by Alexandra Tatu

Dedicated in loving memory of my father,
who inspired me to create.

Harry Amyotte
1962-2018

Here Come the High Notes from FableNotes
Written and created by Marin Marka
Illustrations by Alexandra Tatu

Copyright © 2019 by FableNotes
ISBN 978-1-081-53748-7

All rights reserved.

No part of this publication may be reproduced, distributed or transmitted in any form or by any means, including photocopying, emailing, sharing on social media, scanning, recording, or other electronic or mechanical methods, without the prior written permission of the author, except in the case of brief quotations embodied in critical reviews and certain other noncommercial uses permitted by copyright law.

THE MUSICIAN

thought up many notes,
and the notes made many songs.
But the songs were trapped
inside her head and not
where they belonged.

She drew the notes a treble clef and staff to outline home.

She plopped them on
a Train of Thought
and sent them on their own.

So, off the train came tumbling out the Treble Note Committee.

SNOOTY C
made a great big scene:
he huffed, "I want a throne."

Those lines weren't enough
for C, and so he drew his own.

FRIENDLY D bounced up to C. D asked him "Will you share?"

But Snooty C told Friendly D, "It's *my* line fair and square."

So, up past C went Friendly D to the space below the staff.
D held on tight with all his might, but looked below and gasped!

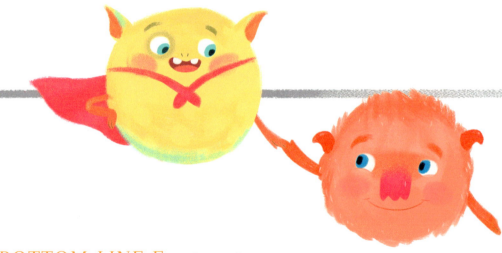

BOTTOM-LINE E, what a hero is she! She gave Friendly D her hand.

Friendly D smiled at Bottom-Line E,
and together they always stand.

SLEEPY F
hung from the clef
scouting for her place.

But she didn't get far before beginning to snore.
So she sleeps in the very first space.

SPEEDY G was so glad to be free,
that she didn't waste any time.

G skipped and stepped past Sleepy F and made it to the second staff line.

PATIENT A marched up and away,
So excited he could burst.

Past C and D, E, F, and G,
A let them all go first.

LITTLE MIDDLE B squeaked, "I want to see!"
So, he followed A up the path.

A gave B a boost on up to line three,
in the middle of the five-line staff.

"Oops!" said C, as she landed on space three, and they both began to laugh.

CLEVER D knew where to be,
so up the staff she rose.

D skipped right past lines E, G, B

to the fourth line that she chose!

CHEERY E skipped merrily up space notes F, A, C.

E skipped once more...

FLYING F
looked up the clef

and waved middle C, "goodbye!"

SNEAKY G
snuck up unseen
as the staff was filling up.

G tiptoed on past everyone to the very tippy top!

The musician watched the Treble Notes as they filled the music sheet.

She heard the happy songs they wrote and tapped her feet to the beat.

The high notes on the treble staff are just where they belong.

So musicians all around the world can play their many songs.

For more fun music learning visit

www.FableNotes.com

Made in United States
Troutdale, OR
09/24/2024